# 40 DAYS OF PRAYER

## FOR MY CHILDREN

CINDY SHUFFLEBARGER

ISBN-13: 978-0-9850049-1-0

# INTRODUCTION

I'm excited you've decided to join this prayer adventure. My hope is that you experience God in a meaningful way over the next 40 days. I pray you renew your hope and faith and that you see new aspects of how God loves you and your children. I trust that He'll meet you right where you are and I pray that you'll overflow with desire to seek Him each day.

I also hope that you'll experience a deeper connection with your children by spending dedicated time in prayer for them. May you celebrate the masterpiece that God is creating before you and cherish them as a gift. May He refresh you and fill you with His peace and joy as you seek Him each day.

Blessings in the journey ahead.

# HOW TO MAKE THE MOST OF THIS JOURNAL

Find a quiet place and begin with a simple prayer asking God to give you insight, wisdom and direction about the topic of the day.

**Verse:**
Read the verse and consider what characteristics of God it reveals.

**Thank you, Lord, for:**
Use this section as praise and thanksgiving.  List attributes of God that you recognize and appreciate.  Or, give thanks for people, provisions, situations, opportunities, solutions, and answers to prayer.

**Prayer:**
Read the prayer and let it be a springboard for your thoughts and conversation with God.  Personalize it beyond the written words.

**Confession:**
Consider any thoughts, attitudes or actions that are interfering with your relationships and ability to parent well. If you're struggling to identify areas that need confession and repentance, ask God to examine your heart.

**Prayers and Reflections:**
Write what comes to mind. Maybe it's a child's name or a trait or issue that you want to commit to pray for. Maybe you write a verse that speaks truth into your circumstances. Or perhaps you want to write out a prayer to God. Each day can look different.

**How I saw evidence of God today:**
Reflecting and recording evidence of God's activity in your life is a helpful reminder that He's always present and at work. Look for ways that you see Him each day. You may see Him evident in His creation, in Scripture, or in your circumstances. Take time to list the ways you see Him.

**More Verses:**
The verses listed in this section offer additional examples and context for the daily topic. Taking time to look them up, either on a Bible app or a hard copy of the Bible, will enrich your quiet time. Make notes about what they mean and specific words or phrases that speak to you. Consider how God is revealing different aspects of Himself through the various verses.

## Wisdom

Verse:

If anyone lacks wisdom, you should ask God, who gives generously to all without finding fault, and it will be given to you.

James 1:5

Thank you, Lord, for:

Prayer:

Dear Father, Please give me wisdom in parenting the children you've entrusted to my care. Help me to see them as Your beautiful creation, fearfully and wonderfully made. Grant my children wisdom as they make choices each day and may Your word be their guide. Amen

Confession:

_____
_____
_____

Date:

## Prayers and Reflections:

_____

_____

_____

_____

_____

_____

_____

_____

_____

_____

_____

**How I saw evidence of God today:**

More Verses: Proverbs 14:1, Ephesians 5:15-16, James 3:17

Verse:

You shall love the Lord your God with all your heart and with all your soul and with all your might.

Deuteronomy 6:5

Thank you, Lord, for:

Prayer:

Dear Father, Draw my children close to You. May they know the depths of your love and grow in their faith and devotion to You. I pray that they seek You to fill their desires and that they worship and praise You daily. Amen

Confession:

_____

_____

_____

Date:

## Prayers and Reflections:

_____

_____

_____

_____

_____

_____

_____

_____

_____

_____

_____

_____

How I saw evidence of God today:

More Verses: Deut 10:12, Psalm 107:8, Matthew 22:36-39

## Uniqueness

**Verse:**

I praise you, for I am fearfully and wonderfully made. Wonderful are your works; my soul knows it very well.

Psalm 139:14

Thank you, Lord, for:

Prayer:

Dear Lord, Please fill my children with the truth of who You created them to be. May they understand that You created them because You love them and have specific work for them. May they celebrate their unique set of qualities and use them to glorify You. Amen.

Confession:

_____

_____

_____

Date:

## Prayers and Reflections:

_____

_____

_____

_____

_____

_____

_____

_____

_____

_____

_____

How I saw evidence of God today:

More Verses: Genesis 1:27, Ephesians 2:10, 1 John 3:1-2

# Gratitude

**Verse:**

Rejoice always, pray
without ceasing, give
thanks in all
circumstances; for this is
the will of God in Christ
Jesus for you.
1 Thess 5:16-18

Thank you, Lord, for:

Prayer:

Lord, Thank you for my children. Help me to model and
teach gratitude through my words and actions. May my
children understand the sacrifice of Your love and truly
appreciate Your gifts. May their hearts be filled with
gratitude. Amen.

Confession:

_____
_____
_____

Date:

## Prayers and Reflections:

_____

_____

_____

_____

_____

_____

_____

_____

_____

_____

_____

How I saw evidence of God today:

More Verses: Psalm 118:24, Psalm 136:1, Colossians 2:6-7

# Worry

**Verse:**

Do not be anxious about anything, but in everything by prayer and supplication with thanksgiving let your requests be made known to God. And the peace of God, which surpasses all understanding, will guard your hearts and your minds in Christ Jesus.
Philippians 4:6-7

Thank you, Lord, for:

**Prayer:**

Father, Help me to trust You with my children – trust that You'll protect them and guide them. Rescue me from my fears and anxiety when I feel inadequate as a parent. Fill me with Your peace today, tomorrow and in the years ahead. I choose to bring everything to You in prayer instead of worrying. Lord, I want to truly rest in Your presence as I walk the journey of parenthood. Amen.

**Confession:**

_____

_____

_____

Date:

## Prayers and Reflections:

_____

_____

_____

_____

_____

_____

_____

_____

_____

_____

_____

_____

How I saw evidence of God today:

More Verses: Proverbs 12:25, John 14:27, 1 Peter 5:7

## Friendship

**Verse:**

Do not be deceived: "Bad company ruins good morals."

1 Corinthians 15:33

**Thank you, Lord, for:**

**Prayer:**

Dear Lord, Please surround my children with people who point them to You. May they choose friends wisely. Give them discernment as they form friendships and may they be good friends in return. Bless them with godly companions. In Jesus' name I ask, Amen.

**Confession:**

_____

_____

_____

Date:

## Prayers and Reflections:

_____

_____

_____

_____

_____

_____

_____

_____

_____

_____

_____

How I saw evidence of God today:

More Verses: Proverbs 1:10-19, Proverbs 4:14-19, 1 Thess 5:11

Verse:

Her children rise up and call her blessed; her husband also, and he praises her.

Proverbs 31:28

Thank you, Lord, for:

Prayer:

Lord, May we appreciate and value family. Help us to model Your love for one another and build healthy, lasting relationships. Bring healing and restoration where necessary. Help us communicate well, serve each other lovingly and enjoy one another. Amen.

Confession:

_____

_____

_____

Date:

## Prayers and Reflections:

_____

_____

_____

_____

_____

_____

_____

_____

_____

_____

_____

How I saw evidence of God today:

More Verses: Exodus 20:22, Joshua 24:15, 1 Timothy 5:8

## Diligence

**Verse:**

Whatever you do, work heartily, as for the Lord and not for men.

Colossians 3:23

**Thank you, Lord, for:**

**Prayer:**

Dear Loving Father, I pray that my children will value hard work and give their best effort in their schoolwork and chores within the home. May they have a helpful attitude and reach the potential you've created in them. Bless their efforts and give them perspective to see the fruit of their work. In Jesus' name I pray, Amen.

**Confession:**

_____

_____

_____

Date:

## Prayers and Reflections:

_____

_____

_____

_____

_____

_____

_____

_____

_____

_____

_____

How I saw evidence of God today:

More Verses: Proverbs 12:24, 1 Cor. 15:58, Hebrews 6:10-12

# Love

**Verse:**
Love is patient and kind; love does not envy or boast; it is not arrogant or rude. It does not insist on its own way; it is not irritable or resentful; it does not rejoice at wrongdoing, but rejoices with the truth. Love bears all things, believes all things, hopes all things, endures all things. Love never ends.
1 Corinthians 13:4-7

**Thank you, Lord, for:**

**Prayer:**
Father, Help me to be a loving example to my children. Help me to see them the way You do and love them abundantly. May I know how to speak their love language and meet their needs accordingly. I also pray that they will be an outpouring of Your love to those around them. May they view others in light of Your truth and show love to all whom they encounter. In Jesus' name, Amen.

**Confession:**

_____

_____

_____

Date:

## Prayers and Reflections:

_____

_____

_____

_____

_____

_____

_____

_____

_____

_____

_____

How I saw evidence of God today:

More Verses: Galatians 5:22-23, Colossians 3:14, 1 John 4:8

## Honesty

**Verse:**

Better is a poor person
who walks in his integrity
than one who is crooked
in speech and is a fool.

Proverbs 19:1

Thank you, Lord, for:

**Prayer:**

Dear Lord, I pray that my children will be truthful in words
and deeds. Protect them from the desire to be deceitful.
Reveal to me when they lie and give me wisdom in how to
deal with dishonest motives. May they have repentant
hearts that want to honor You and may they always feel
safe telling me the truth. Amen.

**Confession:**

_____

_____

_____

Date:

## Prayers and Reflections:

_____

_____

_____

_____

_____

_____

_____

_____

_____

_____

_____

_____

### How I saw evidence of God today:

More Verses: Proverbs 6:16-20, Proverbs 12:22, 1 Peter 3:10-12

## Choices

**Verse:**

So whether we are at home or away, we make it our aim to please him. For we must all appear before the judgment seat of Christ, so that each one may receive what is due for what he has done in the body, whether good or evil.

1 Corinthians 5:9-10

**Thank you, Lord, for:**

**Prayer:**

Father, I pray that my children make choices that honor You and bring blessings instead of despair. May they understand that their choices bring consequences and that they'll be filled with the desire to choose good. Give them the courage and strength to choose Your ways instead of worldly ways. Bless them with wisdom in all things. Amen.

**Confession:**

_____

_____

_____

Date:

Prayers and Reflections:

_____
_____
_____
_____
_____
_____
_____
_____
_____
_____
_____
_____

How I saw evidence of God today:

More Verses: Deut. 28: 1-68, Romans 8:7, Deut. 30:15

# Forgiveness

**Verse:**

If we confess our sins, he is faithful to forgive our sins and to cleanse us from all unrighteousness.

1 John 1:9

**Thank you, Lord, for:**

**Prayer:**

Dear Heavenly Father, Thank you for the gift of forgiveness. May my children be quick to confess sin in their life and seek Your forgiveness and restoration. May they fully understand Your grace and mercy and choose to extend forgiveness to others. Protect them from bitterness and may they be filled grace and love. Amen.

**Confession:**

_____

_____

_____

Date:

## Prayers and Reflections:

_____

_____

_____

_____

_____

_____

_____

_____

_____

_____

_____

How I saw evidence of God today:

More Verses: Matthew 6: 14-15, Mark 11:25, Ephesians 4:32

# Hope

Verse:

"The LORD is my portion," says my soul, "therefore I will hope in him."

Lamentations 3:24

Thank you, Lord, for:

Prayer:

Lord, You are our provider. May my children see evidence of You at work in their lives and be filled with the hope of Your promises. Give them eyes and a heart to see Your perspective and know the truth of Your word. May their hope always come from You and may they always realize their identity as a child of God. In Jesus' name I pray, Amen.

Confession:

_____

_____

_____

Date:

## Prayers and Reflections:

_____
_____
_____
_____
_____
_____
_____
_____
_____
_____
_____

### How I saw evidence of God today:

More Verses: Deuteronomy 31:6, Psalm 43:5, Isaiah 41:10

## Salvation

**Verse:**

For God so loved the world, that he gave his only Son, that whoever believes in him should not perish but have eternal life.
John 3:16

**Thank you, Lord, for:**

**Prayer:**

Dear Loving Father, Draw my children close to you. I pray that they accept Your eternal gift of salvation and walk in their inheritance as a beloved child of God. May they continue to grow in their faith and glorify Your Kingdom. In Jesus' name, Amen.

**Confession:**

_____

_____

_____

Date:

## Prayers and Reflections:

_____

_____

_____

_____

_____

_____

_____

_____

_____

_____

_____

How I saw evidence of God today:

More Verses: Romans 10:9, Ephesians 2:8-9, Titus 3:5

# Generosity

**Verse:**

Give, and it will be given to you. Good measure, pressed down, shaken together, running over, will be put into your lap. For with the measure you use it will be measured back to you."
Luke 6:38

Thank you, Lord, for:

Prayer:

Dear Lord, I pray that my children will be generous with their time, resources and possessions. May they share willingly, help those in need, and not be consumed by materialism. May they understand that all they have comes from You and therefore keep a loose grip on "things", being willing to share and bless others. May I model generosity for them. Thank you for loving us abundantly and providing generously. Amen.

Confession:

_____

_____

_____

Date:

## Prayers and Reflections:

_____

_____

_____

_____

_____

_____

_____

_____

_____

_____

### How I saw evidence of God today:

More Verses: Acts 20:35, 2 Corinthians 9:6-7, 1 John 3:17

## Culture

**Verse:**

Do not be conformed to this world, but be transformed by the renewal of your mind, that by testing you may discern what is the will of God, what is good and acceptable and perfect.
Romans 12:2

Thank you, Lord, for:

**Prayer:**

Father, Protect my children from the effects of this culture and world. I pray that they are consumed by a desire for You instead of worldly things. Draw them close to You and fill them with Your truth. May they hunger and thirst for godly things and reject the temptations of fleeting, temporary things. Guard their hearts and minds and give them a boldness to live for You. Amen.

**Confession:**

_____

_____

_____

Date:

## Prayers and Reflections:

_____

_____

_____

_____

_____

_____

_____

_____

_____

_____

_____

How I saw evidence of God today:

More Verses: 1 Peter 2:9, Titus 2:11-14, 1 John 2:15

## Purpose

**Verse:**

For we are his workmanship, created in Christ Jesus for good works, which God prepared beforehand, that we should walk in them.
Ephesians 2:10

**Thank you, Lord, for:**

**Prayer:**

Dear Father, Help my children understand that You have a calling on their life and have equipped them uniquely. Help me encourage them to find their skills, talents and passion. Help me to provide opportunities for them to explore and reach their potential. May I be their greatest cheerleader and point them to You in all things. Amen

**Confession:**

_____

_____

_____

Date:

## Prayers and Reflections:

_____

_____

_____

_____

_____

_____

_____

_____

_____

_____

_____

_____

How I saw evidence of God today:

More Verses: Isaiah 43:7, Micah 6:8, 1 Corinthians 10:31

## Rest

**Verse:**

Six days you shall work, but on the seventh day you shall rest. In plowing time and in harvest you shall rest.

Exodus 34:21

**Thank you, Lord, for:**

**Prayer:**

Dear Loving Father, Help my children find healthy rhythms in life. May they work hard, but also get adequate rest. Show me how to teach them the principles of a balanced life, putting You first in all things. Fill them with Your peace so their hearts and minds may also rest. May they seek You in all things and truly sense Your presence. In Jesus' name, Amen.

**Confession:**

_____

_____

_____

Date:

## Prayers and Reflections:

_____

_____

_____

_____

_____

_____

_____

_____

_____

_____

_____

How I saw evidence of God today:

More Verses: Psalm 4:8, Jeremiah 31:25, Matthew 11:28-30

## Contentment

Verse:

And my God will supply every need of yours according to his riches in glory in Christ Jesus.

Philippians 4:19

Thank you, Lord, for:

Prayer:

May my children experience contentment regardless of their circumstances or possessions. May they turn to You for their needs and trust that You'll supply every need. Fill them with Your peace and joy that comes from living a life connected to You. In Jesus' name I pray, Amen.

Confession:

_____

_____

_____

Date:

## Prayers and Reflections:

_____

_____

_____

_____

_____

_____

_____

_____

_____

_____

_____

_____

How I saw evidence of God today:

More Verses: 1 Cor. 7:17, Philippians 4:11-12. 1 Tim. 6:6-8

## Priorities

Verse:

But seek first the kingdom of God and his righteousness, and all these things will be added to you.

Matthew 6:33

Thank you, Lord, for:

Prayer:

Lord, I pray that my children will put You above all else. May they run after You with their whole heart, thirsting for You and Your word. Help them to experience the blessings of putting You first and may they seek to honor and glorify You in all things. Amen.

Confession:

_____

_____

_____

Date:

## Prayers and Reflections:

_____

_____

_____

_____

_____

_____

_____

_____

_____

_____

How I saw evidence of God today:

More Verses: Deut 6:5, Luke 10: 38-42, Luke 12:34

## Purity

Verse:

Create in me a clean heart, O God, and renew a right spirit within me.

Psalm 51:10

Thank you, Lord, for:

Prayer:

Lord, I pray that my children will be pure in heart, mind and body. Help them to "flee youthful passions and pursue righteousness, faith, love, and peace, along with those who call on the Lord from a pure heart." (2Tim 2:22) Protect them from harmful images and experiences. Fill them with Your spirit and grace. In Jesus' name, Amen.

Confession:

_____

_____

_____

Date:

## Prayers and Reflections:

_____

_____

_____

_____

_____

_____

_____

_____

_____

_____

_____

How I saw evidence of God today:

More Verses: Proverbs 4:23, Romans 13:14, Colossians 3:5

# Stewardship

**Verse:**

The earth is the LORD's,
and everything in it.
The world and all its
people belong to him.

Psalm 24:1 NLT

**Thank you, Lord, for:**

**Prayer:**
Dear Lord, Help my children to see that all that they have comes from You and that this understanding would motivate them to take care of what they have. From physical possessions to skills and talents, I pray they will develop and use all for Your glory and purposes. May they steward their possessions and resources well and give You the glory and credit for all that they are. Amen.

**Confession:**

_____

_____

_____

Date:

## Prayers and Reflections:

_____

_____

_____

_____

_____

_____

_____

_____

_____

_____

_____

How I saw evidence of God today:

More Verses: Genesis 2:15, Colossians 3:23, 2 Corinthians 9:6-7

Verse:

Blessed are those who hunger and thirst for righteousness, for they shall be satisfied.

Matthew 5:6

Thank you, Lord, for:

Prayer:

Dear Lord, I pray that my children will always have a desire to know You and follow You. May they experience the blessings of Your presence and the riches that come from living a life that glorifies You. Draw them close to You and fill their spirits with Your goodness. May they seek You in all things and know You personally. Amen.

Confession:

_____

_____

_____

Date:

## Prayers and Reflections:

_____
_____
_____
_____
_____
_____
_____
_____
_____
_____
_____
_____
_____

### How I saw evidence of God today:

More Verses: Matthew 7:7, John 6:35, Romans 14:17

## Serving

**Verse:**

As each has received a gift, use it to serve one another, as good stewards of God's varied grace.

1 Peter 4:10

**Thank you, Lord, for:**

**Prayer:**

Dear Father, May my children develop a heart for loving and serving others. Help me to create an environment where this modeled and taught. Show me opportunities to help my children grow in this area and I ask You to place a willing spirit in them. May they understand the value of serving others and view it as an act of worship and blessing to You. Grow their desire to serve, and bless them as they do. Amen.

**Confession:**

_____

_____

_____

Date:

## Prayers and Reflections:

_____

_____

_____

_____

_____

_____

_____

_____

_____

_____

_____

How I saw evidence of God today:

More Verses: Mark 9:35, Galatians 5: 13-14, Philippians 2:1-11

# Fruitfulness

**Verse:**

But the fruit of the Spirit is love, joy, peace, patience, kindness, goodness, faithfulness, gentleness, self-control; against such things there is no law.

Galatians 5:22-23

**Thank you, Lord, for:**

**Prayer:**

Lord, You know my children. I pray that they will respond to Your spirit and produce good fruit. I ask that You work in them in this specific area: _____.
Give them opportunities to practice love, joy, peace, patience, kindness, goodness, faithfulness, gentleness, and self-control. May they grow daily in these areas and be pleasing in Your sight. Thank you for Your goodness and grace. In Jesus' name I pray, Amen.

**Confession:**

_____
_____
_____

Date:

## Prayers and Reflections:

_____
_____
_____
_____
_____
_____
_____
_____
_____
_____
_____
_____

How I saw evidence of God today:

More Verses: John 15:1-17, Romans 7:4, Philippians 1:6

**Verse:**

Sanctify them in the truth; your word is truth.

John 17:17

**Thank you, Lord, for:**

**Prayer:**

Prayer: Lord, Show my children that You and Your word are truth. May they fully understand the importance of standing on Your truth in a culture where truth seems to be relative. May their thoughts and actions be guided by Your truth and may they be blessed abundantly by living according to Your word. Help them to be truthful in all things. In Jesus' name I ask, Amen.

**Confession:**

_____

_____

_____

Date:

## Prayers and Reflections:

_____

_____

_____

_____

_____

_____

_____

_____

_____

_____

_____

How I saw evidence of God today:

More Verses: Proverbs 12:22, John 8:32, 2 Timothy 2:15

# Joy

**Verse:**

May the God of hope fill you with all joy and peace in believing, so that by the power of the Holy Spirit you may abound in hope.

Romans 15:13

**Thank you, Lord, for:**

**Prayer:**

Loving Father, Fill my children with Your joy. Where there is sadness and heartbreak, draw them near to You. May they know the joy of Your presence and choose to meditate on Your goodness instead of the chaos that abounds. Help them to recognize and understand their emotions, but not let their emotions rule and wreck their days. May Your joy in them overflow to those around them, that they may be a light and witness for You. Amen.

**Confession:**

_____

_____

_____

Date:

## Prayers and Reflections:

_____

_____

_____

_____

_____

_____

_____

_____

_____

_____

_____

_____

How I saw evidence of God today:

More Verses: Psalm 16:11, Psalm 118:24, John 15: 1-11

# Future Spouse

**Verse:**

Whoever walks with the wise becomes wise, but the companion of fools will suffer harm.

Proverbs 13:20

Thank you, Lord, for:

Prayer:

Lord, I pray for my child's future spouse. I pray that they are growing in faith and love for You. I pray that You're preparing my child and his/her spouse to be faithful and committed marriage partners. May they choose to love sacrificially. Give them the wisdom to recognize each other when the time comes and may they strengthen and complement each other as they do life together. Most of all, may You be at the center of their relationship. Amen.

Confession:

_____

_____

_____

Date:

## Prayers and Reflections:

_____

_____

_____

_____

_____

_____

_____

_____

_____

_____

_____

_____

### How I saw evidence of God today:

More Verses: 2 Corinthians 6:14, Eph. 5:33, Colossians 3:18-19

## Emotional Health

**Verse:**

Finally, brothers, whatever is true, whatever is honorable, whatever is just, whatever is pure, whatever is lovely, whatever is commendable, if there is any excellence, if there is anything worthy of praise, think about these things.

Philippians 4:8

**Thank you, Lord, for:**

**Prayer:**

Dear Lord, I pray for the emotional health of my children. May they acknowledge their emotions but not be ruled by them. May they find confidence, peace and worth in You. Guard their hearts and minds from the enemy's lies and show them Your truth in every circumstance. In Jesus' name I ask, Amen.

**Confession:**

_____

_____

_____

Date:

## Prayers and Reflections:

_____

_____

_____

_____

_____

_____

_____

_____

_____

_____

_____

How I saw evidence of God today:

More Verses: Isaiah 26:3, Romans 12:2, Philippians 4:6-7

## Worship

**Verse:**

I appeal to you therefore, brothers, by the mercies of God, to present your bodies as a living sacrifice, holy and acceptable to God, which is your spiritual worship.
Romans 12:1

Thank you, Lord, for:

Prayer:

Lord, You are worthy of all praise. I pray that my children will praise You in every season of their lives. May we stay focused on You and Your ways and may we worship You in thoughts and actions. May our lives reflect You and bring You glory. We love You and praise you. Amen.

Confession:

_____

_____

_____

Date:

Prayers and Reflections:

_____

_____

_____

_____

_____

_____

_____

_____

_____

_____

_____

How I saw evidence of God today:

More Verses: Psalm 95: 1-6, Isaiah 12:5, 1 Peter 2:9

## Grace

**Verse:**

Let us then with confidence draw near to the throne of grace, that we may receive mercy and find grace to help in time of need.

Hebrews 4:16

**Thank you, Lord, for:**

**Prayer:**

Dear Lord, I need your grace as I parent my children. Likewise, I pray that they experience and understand Your grace. Work gently in them to accomplish Your goals and give them strength to choose wisely and to love and serve others. I pray that they'll extend grace to those around them and be an instrument of Your love. Thank you, Jesus.

**Confession:**

_____

_____

_____

Date:

## Prayers and Reflections:

_____

_____

_____

_____

_____

_____

_____

_____

_____

_____

_____

How I saw evidence of God today:

More Verses: 2 Corinthians 12:9, Colossians 4:2-6, James 4:6

## Mercy

**Verse:**

But God, being rich in mercy, because of the great love with which he loved us, even when we were dead in our trespasses, made us alive together with Christ—by grace you have been saved.
Ephesians 2:4-5

**Thank you, Lord, for:**

**Prayer:**

Father, Thank you that You're gracious and merciful. I pray that my children experience your mercy in situations where they fail. I pray they experience Your mercy when they're unaware of their need. And, Lord, I pray they receive Your mercy with thanksgiving and gratitude. May they extend mercy and grace to those around them as an outpouring of Your love. In Jesus' name I ask, Amen.

**Confession:**

_____

_____

_____

Date:

Prayers and Reflections:

_____

_____

_____

_____

_____

_____

_____

_____

_____

_____

_____

How I saw evidence of God today:

More Verses: Psalm 86:5, Luke 6:36, James 2:13

# Abide

**Verse:**

I am the vine; you are the branches. Whoever abides in me and I in him, he it is that bears much fruit, for apart from me you can do nothing.

John 15:5

**Thank you, Lord, for:**

**Prayer:**

Lord, Help me to stay focused on You as I parent. Renew me daily and fill me with Your joy and strength. I pray that my children grow in their relationship with You and lead fruitful lives. May they know You in a personal way and experience Your love and presence in each day. Guide them and draw them near to You. In Jesus' name, Amen.

**Confession:**

_____

_____

_____

Date:

## Prayers and Reflections:

_____

_____

_____

_____

_____

_____

_____

_____

_____

_____

_____

How I saw evidence of God today:

More Verses: Psalm 119, Jeremiah 29: 11-13, John 15: 1-17

Verse:

Let each of you look not only to his own interests, but also to the interests of others.

Philippians 2:4

Thank you, Lord, for:

Prayer:
Loving Father, I pray that my children will notice others and look for ways to encourage. Help them to see the needs of those around them and find ways to help. May they be outwardly focused instead of focused on themselves. Lord, use them to show Your love and make the world a better place. May they share Your blessings with others. Thank you for loving us generously. Amen.

Confession:

_____

_____

_____

Date:

## Prayers and Reflections:

_____

_____

_____

_____

_____

_____

_____

_____

_____

_____

_____

### How I saw evidence of God today:

More Verses: Luke 6:38, Romans 12:10, 1 John 4:19

# Encouragement

**Verse:**

Let no corrupting talk come out of your mouths, but only such as is good for building up, as fits the occasion, that it may give grace to those who hear.
Ephesians 4:29

**Thank you, Lord, for:**

**Prayer:**

Dear Father, Please let me be an encouragement to my children. Help me to recognize when they need it most and give me the wisdom to know how to best encourage. May they also receive encouragement from Your Word and then encourage those around them. May their words be wholesome and build up others. May their attitudes and actions be pleasing to You. I praise you for the ways You are at work in our lives. Amen.

**Confession:**

_____

_____

_____

Date:

## Prayers and Reflections:

_____

_____

_____

_____

_____

_____

_____

_____

_____

_____

_____

How I saw evidence of God today:

More Verses: Isaiah 40: 30-31, 1 Thess 5:11, Hebrews 10:24-25

## Courage

**Verse:**

Have I not commanded you? Be strong and courageous. Do not be frightened, and do not be dismayed, for the LORD your God is with you wherever you go.

Joshua 1:9

**Thank you, Lord, for:**

**Prayer:**

Father, Fill my children with courage as they follow Your ways. Fill them with Your truth, that they may stand for what is right in Your eyes. I pray that they'll be quick to defend those that need defending, that they'll be a friend to those who need a friend, and that they'll include those who are different and alone. Give them the courage to show love to others. Use them for Your glory. Amen.

**Confession:**

_____

_____

_____

Date:

## Prayers and Reflections:

_____

_____

_____

_____

_____

_____

_____

_____

_____

_____

_____

How I saw evidence of God today:

More Verses: Deuteronomy 31:6, Psalm 27:14, 2 Timothy 1:7

## Patience

Verse:

Be still before the
Lord and wait patiently
for him.

Psalm 37:7

Thank you, Lord, for:

Prayer:

Dear Loving Father, Thank you for your patience with me.
Help me extend the same patience to my children.
Likewise, may they grow in patience. Teach them to be
patient with themselves and others. As they grow and
mature, help them to wait patiently for You instead of
running ahead of Your plans. I thank you for Your grace
and love. Amen.

Confession:

_____

_____

_____

Date:

## Prayers and Reflections:

_____

_____

_____

_____

_____

_____

_____

_____

_____

_____

_____

How I saw evidence of God today:

More Verses: Galatians 6:9, Colossians 3:12, James 1:19

# Protection

Verse:

Keep me as the apple of your eye; hide me in the shadow of your wings.

Psalm 17:8

Thank you, Lord, for:

Prayer:
Lord, Please protect my children from harm – physical and emotional. Guard them from illness and injury. Shelter their hearts and minds from the lies of the enemy. May they be healthy in mind, body and spirit. Help them to make good choices that lead to life and health instead of destruction and detriment. Reveal to me where I should intervene and give me wisdom in how I parent. Amen.

Confession:

_____
_____
_____

Date:

## Prayers and Reflections:

_____

_____

_____

_____

_____

_____

_____

_____

_____

_____

How I saw evidence of God today:

More Verses: Psalm 91:1-2, Isaiah 41:10, 2 Thessalonians 3:3

# Healing

**Verse:**

Behold, I will bring to it health and healing, and I will heal them and reveal to them abundance of prosperity and security.

Jeremiah 33:6

**Thank you, Lord, for:**

**Prayer:**

Dear Jesus, Please bring healing to my children where it's needed. Bring to my attention any emotional or physical needs my child has. Equip me to love them through their struggles with wisdom and grace. Tend to their every need, especially those of which I am unaware. Free them from past hurts and show them the path forward. May they experience Your grace and love in each day. Amen.

**Confession:**

Date:

## Prayers and Reflections:

_____
_____
_____
_____
_____
_____
_____
_____
_____
_____
_____

How I saw evidence of God today:

More Verses: Psalm 102: 2-4, Psalm 147: 3, Isaiah 61:7-8

## Blessings

**Verse:**

The LORD bless you and keep you; the LORD make his face to shine upon you and be gracious to you; the LORD lift up his countenance upon you and give you peace. Numbers 6:24-26

**Thank you, Lord, for:**

**Prayer:**

Dear Gracious Lord, Thank you for the ways You bless us. I ask each of those blessings for my children. May they prosper in their relationships, may they know the depths of Your love, may they have an abundance of peace. Lord, I ask You to bless them beyond anything I can ask or imagine and that they'll love You and serve You all the days of their lives. In Jesus' name I ask, Amen.

**Confession:**

_____

_____

_____

Date:

## Prayers and Reflections:

---------------------------------
---------------------------------
---------------------------------
---------------------------------
---------------------------------
---------------------------------
---------------------------------
---------------------------------
---------------------------------
---------------------------------
---------------------------------

**How I saw evidence of God today:**

More Verses: 2 Corinthians 9:8, Ephesians, 1:3, James 1:17

Dear Sweet Friend,

Keep praying for your children.  It will always be time well spent.  And while you may not see immediate outcomes, know that God is at work in their lives and yours.  He created your children and placed them with you – not by accident but with full knowledge and intentionality. Rest in His peace as you draw on His strength to parent them.

Grace and peace,
*Cindy*

P.S. I love to hear stories of God at work. If you'd like to share something you've experienced during the past 40 days of working through this journal, feel free to email me at cindy@cindyshufflebarger.com.

Made in the USA
Middletown, DE
10 October 2018